Horoscopes

Reality
Or
Trickery?

Book one in the
Sleuthing for Explanations series.

By Kimberly Blaker

Illustrations by Diana Silkina
Cover illustrations by Cassie King

Green Grove Press
Farmington Hills, Michigan

Copyright © 2018 by Kimberly Blaker

All rights reserved

Published by Green Grove Press,
P.O. Box 3497, Farmington Hills, Michigan 48334

Website: www.greengrovepress.com

Printed and bound in the United States

Cover illustrations by Cassie King
Cover design by Kimberly Blaker

Library of Congress Control Number: 2018901797

ISBN: 978-0-9725496-6-0 (Cloth)
ISBN: 978-0-9725496-7-7 (Paper)
ISBN: 978-0-9725496-8-4 (Electronic)

Horoscopes: Reality or Trickery?

To Skyla & Zayne –

Who will soon
be old enough
to read this.

Table of Contents

INTRODUCTION

Have you ever read your horoscope and it seemed so true it had to be written for you?

Today I looked up my own horoscope. It read:

> Your attention could be focused on getting your work duties done efficiently today. The desire to be organized may be due to your self-discipline and motivation to be the best at what you do. Avoiding distractions might be a way to maintain your concentration and stay on track today. If you are often interrupted at work, perhaps you can let others know that you would like to be disturbed only in an emergency. Likewise if your mind has the tendency to wander, you might want to pretend that you are in a remote place far from everything--phones, computers, or people--that might disturb you. Imagining that you are secluded from others for a short while could give you both the physical and mental privacy you need to tend to your responsibilities.[1]

I thought, wow! That seems so true. I do have a lot of self-discipline and motivation to be the best I can be in everything I do. I'm a freelance writer, and I work out of

Horoscopes: Reality or Trickery?

an office at home. I work long hard hours to meet my deadlines and achieve my goals.

At the same time, I often have difficulty focusing. That's because I have a 3-year-old bullmastiff dog named Boudica. My 115-pound pooch usually spends much of the day pestering me to play with her and for treats. Do you have a dog? If so, you probably know just what I mean. But despite her usual interruptions, I've been really focused today on getting my work done.

In fact, this morning Boudica (or Puppenstuff, as I affectionately call her) interrupted me about five times within a short time. So, I asked her to please give me a break today—as if she could understand me. But it worked! From that point on, she let up. Then I put on my invisible blinders to block out all the other distractions in my surroundings. As a result, I was able to tend to my responsibilities—just as my horoscope predicted I'd be able to do.

Do you wonder, though, if there's a scientific explanation for why my horoscope seemed so true?

Through the rest of this book you're going to uncover a lot of fascinating facts about horoscopes and astrology as you sleuth for answers to this question and many more. Then, towards the end of the book, you can also do experiments and activities of your own to help you determine for yourself whether astrology is real or just a hoax.

CHAPTER 1

WHAT EXACTLY *ARE* ASTROLOGY, HOROSCOPES, AND ZODIAC SIGNS?

Astrology is the study of how the movements of the sun, moon, planets, and stars influence human behavior and events. Astrologers say the position of the planets and stars when you were born determines your personality and your future. The movements of these bodies right after your birth are important, too. What do you think? Could something light-years away affect who you are and everything you do in life?

Ancient beginnings

The reason astrology came about is that ancient people wanted to understand happenings they couldn't explain. But how and when did astrology begin?

Archaeologists don't have all the answers. What they do know is astrology developed in different civilizations. Archaeologists also know astrology was practiced at least as early as 3000 BC. That's about 5,000 years ago!

Babylonia is one of the oldest civilizations recognized as developing the practice. Around 2000 BC the Chinese were also practicing astrology. These early people probably first discovered the bodies in the sky were directly related to changes in seasons. Babylonian priests

recorded the movements in the skies. Then they recorded the events that took place on earth at the same time. The priests related the heavenly and earthly events to each other.

Babylonians developed a reasonably accurate calendar as well. It was based on the movements in the skies. This allowed astrologers to combine mathematics and observations. These were used to predict the movements of the planets.

A valuable tool

The movement of astronomical bodies came to be significant in many ways. The orbit of the sun was most important. That's because it affected crops. So, astrology became a guide for when to plant and when to harvest— and it worked!

Planting according to the movement of the sun makes sense. Most often, it's best to plant during the spring. That's because as summer approaches the sun hits the earth at an increasingly steeper angle. This increases the amount of energy that hits any particular spot on the earth. This, combined with longer daylight hours, helps the earth to warm up more. All of this helps crops to grow.

The planets also seemed to affect war. A wise man associated red with bloodshed and bloodshed with war. So, when Nergal, or Mars, was at its brightest, it meant war would take place. This seemed quite reasonable to people during those times. That's because Mars was frequently bright—and battles were frequent, too. Can you see how the frequency of these two events and the coincidence of them often coinciding could have led people to believe they were associated?

Omen astrology

During the early days of astrology, the practice was used to make predictions that would affect the state. This often meant making predictions for kings, too, because of the importance of forecasts to the country.

Martian skies

Nergal, the planet that we now know as Mars, is known as the Red Planet. That's because it has red dirt. The sky of Mars is pink because the wind blows around the Martian dust.

This early form of astrology is sometimes referred to as omen astrology. Omen astrology predicted only significant events. Predictions of personalities and happenings for ordinary people were not made during these ancient times.

Along comes the Zodiac

Around 600 to 300 BC, all of this changed. First, the zodiac was developed to measure time.

The zodiac is a circle containing twelve constellations or patterns of stars. The circle represents a path. Early astronomers and astrologers believed the sun took this route as it traveled around the earth.

Each constellation, or zodiac sign, along the path represents 30 days. Twelve constellations times 30 days equals 360 days. That's nearly one year for the sun to make its way around the earth.

What's your sign?

Are you familiar with the zodiac signs? You might recognize the names: Aquarius, Pisces, Aries, Taurus, Gemini, Cancer, Leo, Virgo, Libra, Scorpio, Sagittarius, and Capricorn.

Whichever constellation the sun is in at your time of birth determines your zodiac sign. Can you find which sign is yours? Look for the one in which your birthday falls.

Horoscope astrology begins

After the zodiac was developed, horoscope

Sun signs

Zodiac signs are also known as sun signs. They take their names from constellations or groups of stars. Each zodiac sign is assigned certain dates based on when the sun passes through a constellation.

The belt of the animals

The word *zodiac* comes from the Greek *zodiakos*. Zodiakos kyklos means 'circle of animals. The name was given because the regions of the constellations are connected to each other in the sky. Either animals or people are what eleven of the twelve signs are named after.

astrology began. Horoscope astrology is the foretelling of events based on peoples' date and time of birth.

Horoscopes are the charts that are used by astrologers. These charts show the position of the planets and the stars at particular times. Specific human characteristics have been assigned to each zodiac sign. Astrologers use these charts to determine your character and to tell your future.

Most of us are not familiar with horoscopes in the same way as astrologers. But horoscopes are also the astrological forecasts that you read in magazines, newspapers, and online.

You've probably seen these. They are categorized by zodiac signs and their corresponding dates. Underneath the zodiac sign, there is usually a paragraph or more describing your personality and offering predictions and advice.

A universal system

Today, most astrologers follow Ptolemaic astrology. Claudius Ptolemy lived around 100 A.D. He contributed significantly to astrology by studying the different forms that were practiced. Ptolemy organized

Earth is the center of the universe? Ptolemy also asserted that the earth is the center of the universe and that the stars circle the earth. Today, we know otherwise.

The Twelve Zodiac Signs

Aquarius
January 20 -
February 18

Pisces
February 19 -
March 20

Aries
March 21 -
April 19

Taurus
April 20 -
May 20

Gemini
May 21 -
June 20

Cancer
June 21 -
July 22

Leo
July 23 -
August 22

Virgo
August 23 -
September 22

Libra
September 23 -
October 22

Scorpio
October 23 -
November 21

Saggitarius
November 22 -
December 21

Capricorn
December 22
- January 19

these different systems into one. Then he wrote books that explained the new system.

Astronomy versus astrology

Eventually, the science of astronomy developed out of astrology. Astronomy is the study of all celestial bodies in the universe. Astrologers used scientific observations and math for charting constellations and the sun and moon. Some ancient people were both astrologers *and* astronomers.

But astronomy is different from astrology. Astronomy is concerned with learning what the different bodies are in the sky and measuring and explaining their movements.

Still, astrology and astronomy went hand in hand in those early days. It wasn't until famous astronomers came along like Galileo Galilei and Nicolaus Copernicus that this all changed. These men made huge claims that put astrology to the test.

A most important realization by Copernicus was that the earth revolves around the sun. In other words, the earth is *not* the center of the universe.

In the early 1600s, Galileo built his very own telescope. He used it to verify Copernicus's claim.

Where scientists stand today

Since around the 1500s, not many scientists have accepted astrology as science. Some even argue that astrology grew into a form of magic based on superstition.

Still, astronomers have taken some very useful things from astrology. Ancient astrologers gave names to the groupings of stars. This makes it easy for astronomers to find objects in the sky.

A vision of light

Try this! After sunset or just before the morning twilight, see if you can see the zodiacal light that is sometimes visible on the horizon. The faint band of zodiacal light stretches across the path of the planets. The best place to see it is in a dark place away from city lights. The best time to view it is in the spring. The light is created from dust particles from comets and asteroids. Sunlight makes the particles visible as the light hits and bounces off the particles.

CHAPTER 2

WHAT'S THE EVIDENCE FOR ASTROLOGY?

There are many arguments both for and against the validity of astrology. So, let's look at both sides. Then we'll weigh out the evidence.

Could millions of people be wrong?

Astrologers say one reason astrology must be valid is that so many people believe in it. It's true a lot of people do believe in it. In fact, many famous and important people believe in astrology, too. Not only that, but people have accepted it for thousands of years.

Is it possible so many people could be wrong?

Think of this. What if I said an invisible fairy named Twinkledust lives right in my bottom desk drawer? Suppose I tell this to many people, and many of those people believe me. Would that make it true?

The science behind astrology

Astrologers say that tides are also evidence that planets and stars influence events on earth. They're right!

The moon and sun affect earth because they're so near to us. Gravity from the sun, but primarily the moon causes the tides to rise and fall. The moon creates a gravitational force that pulls upward the ocean's water causing it to bulge. As a result, the tides rise both where the earth faces the moon and on the opposite side of the earth. Then, as the earth rotates, the areas where the tide had risen begin to recede, also known as low tide. So, there's a scientific explanation for the tides.

There are many ways that the sun affects the earth as well. Even though the sun is 93 million miles away, the movement of the earth around this massive star gives our planet light.

At the sun's center, it is 27 million degrees Fahrenheit. That's 13,500 times hotter than a chimney gets during a fire in a fireplace. So, even at such distance, the sun can provide heat for our planet.

The earth's orbit around the sun causes changes in seasons, as well. And earth's plant and animal life are all dependent on the sun for energy.

Galileo on astronomical bodies

Even Galileo recognized the effects of the sun on earth. He once remarked about this magnificent star:

> The Sun, with all the planets revolving around it, and depending on it, can still ripen a bunch of grapes as though it had nothing else in the Universe to do.

Galileo was right. The sun affects so many things on earth, from the paramount to the least significant.

So, in many ways, astrologers are correct when they say that astrological bodies affect happenings here on earth. But there are also scientific explanations with the events I've discussed so far.

How about the planets?

Scientists say that the distance of the other planets from earth makes it unlikely that those planets have any effect. Scientists agree that the sun and the moon affect the earth. But scientists dispute that the bodies in the sky affect people's personalities and life events.

What do you think? Do the moon and sun's effects on earth necessarily mean that the sun, moon, planets, and stars affect people's personalities and their future?

Judging astrology

Astrologers insist that people who are not astrologers are not qualified to judge astrology. Maybe they have a point. If we don't have expertise in something, do we have the ability to determine if it works? Let's examine this argument.

Imagine your new teacher, Ms. Smartypants, tells you she has a new method for teaching math. Instead of showing you examples on the chalkboard, she's going to let your brain teach itself. The reason for using this technique, says Ms. Smartypants, is simple! It's because it works.

Next, Ms. Smartypants passes out a worksheet with several math problems. You and your classmates skim the worksheet in total bewilderment. You've never seen this type of problem before. But that doesn't matter, your teacher insists, as she announces it's time to get started.

After several days of using this new method, you and your classmates are stumped! You've still not figured out how to do the math problems, let alone where to begin.

Are you qualified to judge this new teaching method even though you're not a teacher yourself?

Are you aware of the effect this method has on *your* ability to learn the math? Can you observe the effect this technique has on *other* students' ability to learn the material?

What about your parents? They are neither teachers *nor* students. Does this mean they are unable to make an accurate judgment about the teaching method?

Maybe you don't need to be a teacher to study the effectiveness of the method after all—or to judge if the claim is valid. It would be a crazy world if judgment of something could only come from those who practice or believe in it.

Beware of the full moon

Have you ever heard that when there's a full moon, the crazies come out? Many astrologers believe this is true. That's because people have done bad and crazy things when there is a full moon. And there are documented cases to prove it! Astrologers say this is evidence that the planets and stars affect human behavior.

But it turns out data have shown astrologers are mistaken. People do bad things just as often when there is a quarter moon or a half moon. It is only an illusion that people do crazy things because of the full moon.

That's because when the moon is full, it stands out. If someone does something crazy when there's a full moon, people tend to notice the moon. But, on nights when the moon isn't full and something bad happens, people don't pay attention to its size.

Think of it this way. Have you ever had a haircut and everyone noticed it? That's probably because the style or length was very different from what it usually is.

What about a haircut that no one noticed? That most likely occurred because your hairstyle wasn't a big change. We're more likely to notice things that are obvious, different, or infrequent.

That's the way it is with a full moon. It is obvious and is infrequent.

Astrology Works⁉!

Pioneer astrologer Grant Lewi said, "Astrology is valid for the same reason the multiplication table is valid —because it works."[2]

That astrology works is a common argument offered by astrologers and those who follow astrology. At first glance, this only stands to reason.

But this statement is called "begging the question." This means that the support for the claim is just a restatement of the claim itself. Saying that astrology is "valid" and that it "works" is the same thing. It doesn't offer us any *proof* that it works.

There are other errors in the astrologer's statement as well. For example, multiplication tables work every time. Three times three is always nine.

Yet, astrology only "works" some of the time. In fact, the more precise the predictions, the higher the failure rate.

Generalizations in astrology are sort of like the generalization "a number times a number equals a number." Indeed, such a vague statement assures that it will be correct or perceived as right. But, when forecasts become specific, as are multiplication tables, astrology is often in error.

Living proof

Astrologers also say astrology works because there are testimonials to prove it. So, how can scientists say that it doesn't?

This is a tricky argument. Imagine you have a headache and decide there has to be a better way to cure it than to swallow a yucky pill. So, you decide to experiment with some of your favorite treats. It would be just awesome to find something tasty to eliminate aches and pains.

First, you try a Popsicle. But a little while later, your head is still pounding.

Next, you try a few chocolate chips your mom hid in the back of a cupboard. Twenty minutes later, your head is feeling no better.

So, you decide to make a glass of sugar water. Soon, your headache goes away. You're sure the sugar water was the cure. Who could argue? You have a testimonial to prove it!

Are you thinking what I'm thinking? Could it be a coincidence your headache went away after drinking the sugar water? Maybe your headache just finally ran its course and went away on its own.

Is it possible then that testimonials for astrology could also be a coincidence? What if your horoscope predicted, "Something good is going to come your way today"? There is a reasonable chance of it being accurate.

Something good happens to most people almost every day, even if it's as ordinary as getting to hang out with a best friend or making a good grade on a test. Now, everyone who had something good come his or her way has a testimonial. Do those testimonials automatically mean that astrology is valid? Or could there be alternative reasons the predictions were correct?

Mind games

Maybe your mind even played a trick on you. Sometimes when we want something to be true, our minds can convince ourselves it's so. Sometimes we make things happen subconsciously. That means the back of our mind is thinking and causing us to act in a manner or for reasons we don't even realize. This is referred to as the self-fulfilling prophecy.

A look at science

Fortunately, many scientific studies have been conducted on astrology. Scientific studies make it possible to examine a claim and determine its validity.

Criteria for science

There are several important criteria for science.

First, there must be a *natural* cause that explains the happening. In science, supernatural causes cannot be used to explain something.

Second, it must be possible to *observe* and explain the event by using one of our senses: hearing, seeing, smelling, touching, or tasting. Tools that assist our senses, such as a microscope, can also be used.

Next, it must be possible to make specific *predictions* about the natural cause.

Fourth, the cause of the happening must be *testable*. In science, tests must be controlled for accuracy, and the scientific method must be used.

Fifth, results from testing must be *consistent*. This means it must be possible to do the same test repeatedly. And each time, the results must be very much the same.

Finally, scientific theories are *tentative*. As we learn more about something, the theory must be changed based on new understandings.

Putting astrology to the test

With a basic understanding of science, let's look at some studies. Many studies have been conducted to determine if astrology is valid.

> A **correlation** means there is a relationship between two things. But a correlation doesn't necessarily mean one is the cause of the other.

A couple of studies astrologers sometimes refer to found there's a correlation between astrological bodies and people who are introverted or extraverted. These studies were conducted in 1978 and 1979[3], but astrologers still refer to them today.

> A person who's shy, reserved, and turns inward is considered an **introvert**. Someone who's outgoing and turns outward is called an **extravert**.

But then a third identical study was conducted in 1979. Only in this study, the results were very different, and no correlation was found.[4]

Do you remember one of the criteria for science is consistency? In other words, identical tests should have similar results. So, an error must have occurred either in the first two experiments or the third one.

And that's precisely what was found. Other researchers discovered a big error in the first two studies. In those studies, some of the test subjects were very familiar with astrology. They already knew the characteristics assigned to their zodiac sign. It's likely their knowledge this affected some of their responses during testing.[5]

That's why scientific studies must be controlled. Anything that might affect the outcome of a study must be recognized. Then such factors must either be eliminated or adjusted so as not to affect the outcome.

Researcher gets opposite results

Over the next three years, three different kinds of studies were conducted. These studies found no relationship between personality and zodiac signs.[6] This again included the characteristics of extraversion and introversion.

Also, of interest, one of the researchers of one of these later studies had conducted one of the first two studies in which a correlation had initially been found. In his new study, Eysenck found no correlation between astrological bodies and extraversion or introversion.[7]

The Mars effect

Another study astrologers say supports astrology is referred to as Gauquelin's "Mars Effect." That's because in 1955, a French psychologist, Michel Gauquelin made an exciting discovery. He analyzed data and found a small correlation between being a great athlete and the position of Mars at the time of birth. He discovered only 17% of the general population was born during key Mars sectors. Yet, 22% of outstanding sports champions were born during these sectors.[8]

For many years, there was a big debate over whether this study was valid. In fact, following a test known as 'the Zelen test,' it seemed there might be some truth to the Mars effect. The Zelen test confirmed just under 17% of the general population was born during key Mars sectors.

But finally, a new study in 1979 to 1980 was reported. The results of this study found only 18.66% of outstanding sports champions were born during key Mars sectors. So it turns out, the difference between the general population and star athletes is too insignificant to have any meaning.[9]

This led to further review of Gauquelin's database, which had been used to determine the Mars effect. It was discovered that there had been numerous discrepancies. As a result, the original findings were in error.[10]

In the majority

Of the numerous studies that have been conducted on astrology, most have found no correlation between astrological bodies and personality or life events.

One such study reviewed the sun signs of 6,000 politicians and 10,000 scientists. It found the zodiac signs were divided about equally among the politicians and scientists. No correlation was found between peoples' professions and their zodiac signs.[11]

Putting accuracy to the test

In another interesting study, researchers reviewed 3,000 predictions made by famous astrologers. Only 10% of the predictions came true. That's just one out of every ten. Even the few predictions that did seem accurate were usually vague. In other cases, anyone could have guessed the outcome based on current events.[12]

Studies have also been conducted to determine the relationship between astrological bodies and peoples' height, occupation, and life expectancy. But they've found no correlation.

Interestingly, a study reported in a 2015 medical journal found there is some relationship between the month of birth and health. For example, it found people born in October and November were at higher risk for neurological, respiratory, and reproductive illnesses. But researchers believe this has less to do with astrology and more to do with the environment into which children are born. Here's an excellent example of the environmental factor based on month or season of birth. Babies born during a time of year when there are more dust mites in the home are more likely to develop asthma.[13]

Even Grant Lewi, the astrologer, agreed that astrology couldn't predict careers. He said astrology could only indicate personality traits such as artistic temperament, "a matter-of-fact approach to life," or a keen interest in new and modern things.[14]

Of course, these traits are quite general and can be seen in most people in one way or another regardless of their astrological symbol. And as I mentioned, studies haven't found any support for Lewi's claim regarding personality traits.

Is marriage written in the stars?

Perhaps the largest study on astrology ever was conducted by David Voas. Astrologers claim people with certain zodiac signs are more compatible with each other and more likely to marry each other. For example, Capricorns are more compatible with Taurus according to astrologers. So Voas used the 2001 census of England and Wales and reviewed the birth dates and zodiac signs of 20 million married people. It turns out there's no tendency for people to marry those who are more compatible with their own zodiac signs.[15]

Consumers beware!

One scientist came up with this unique study. First, he advertised in a newspaper offering a free horoscope just for the asking. In response, he received letters from 150 people who provided him their time and place of birth, as requested.

Next, the scientist mailed the same horoscope to each person. He included a questionnaire for each person to return.

What was the result? Ninety-four percent of the recipients who wrote back admitted they recognized themselves in the horoscope.

Now here's the twist. Little did these people know, the horoscope had been written for a French serial killer![16]

Expert confusion

In another study, researchers consulted with six expert astrologers. An individual who was to impersonate an astrologer was also enlisted for the study.

For the experiment, the experts and impersonator were asked to identify which of 23 astrological birth charts belonged to which of 23 people. To be able to do so, the astrologers were given a file with a great deal of information about each person.

In the end, the astrologers did no better at matching up people to their astrological birth charts than did the impersonator. The six *real* astrologers also could not even agree with each other on which chart belonged to which person.[17]

The odds are....

A well-known study was conducted in 1985 by astrophysicist Shawn Carlson. He located 28 of the highest rated astrologers from America and Europe. Then he asked 116 people to fill out a personality inventory.

For each person, an astrologer was given the person's birth information. Each astrologer was also given three personality surveys from which to choose. Only one survey was the correct one for the person whose birth information he received. Astrologers had a 1 in 3 chance of being right by just making a wild guess. Finally, even *after* studying the surveys, the astrologers were correct only 1 out of every three times.[18] This means they were no more accurate than non-astrologers would have been who merely guessed.

Problems in the stars

There's another reason scientists say astrology is invalid as well. The position of the sun has shifted since astrology was first developed. It has shifted so much, in fact, that it's off by one full constellation or zodiac sign.

In other words, the position of the sun in the constellations on June 15, 2017, is not the same as it was on June 15, 200. This is because the sun, in relation to the constellations, is not constant. So, the zodiac signs no longer coordinate with the dates that were assigned to them.[19]

Yet, astrologers haven't adjusted the dates for the sun signs. Neither have they adjusted for this in their practice.

CHAPTER 3

HOW ARE HOROSCOPES CREATED?

Astrologers say our personality, behavior, and all aspects of life are determined by the position of the sun, moon, planets, and stars when we were born. Astrologers make mathematical computations to come up with horoscopes. These calculations are based on movements of the astrological bodies and where they are in relation to other stars and planets at particular times.

The accuracy of astrologers' predictions varies. Usually, the more detailed the prediction, the less likely it is to be accurate. That's why astrologers must use a variety of techniques to make their predictions seem accurate.

Specifics versus generalizations

The most common technique astrologers use is making vague statements. They make predictions and give few, if any, details about the forecast.

An astrologer might predict: "You will have a visitor today."

This prediction is likely to come true because *many* people will have a visitor on any given day.

Horoscope readers will accept the prediction as true even if the visitor is just a neighbor who stopped outside

to chat for a minute or a postal worker delivering a package.

In reality, the statement will also be true for just as many people under a different zodiac sign. Still, the prediction was not made for these other people.

All in the mind

Authors of an article appearing in the journal *Astronomy* say, "Most astrologers today are amateur psychologists—their horoscope readings and newspaper descriptions are vague and reassuring."[20] This is certainly true.

Still, many astrologers believe wholeheartedly in what they're doing. Many are probably not in the business to deceive people. They're certain they're helping others by offering predictions and advice.

But most astrologers have at least some understanding of psychology. Some have even studied it extensively. They know how our minds work and how to make their predictions believable. Many astrologers may believe so strongly in astrology they don't even realize they're using methods that might be considered trickery.

And today's forecast is...

Another technique astrologers use is to make predictions based on current events or forecasts. A horoscope might suggest: "Rain is in your forecast for today."

The astrologer probably looked at the weather forecast before making the prediction and knew there was a good chance of rain. But this statement would apply to people of all other zodiac signs as well.

If the prediction is wrong and it doesn't rain, the statement can still be perceived another way. The reader might think of it as a colorful way of saying the reader is going to have a bad day. The statement will be true for many people because of the probability of rain and the number of people who will have a bad day.

Body talk

Astrologers, like other fortunetellers, have advantages when they offer individualized charts and consultations. Astrologers are experts on body language, which is an area of psychology. They can look at your clothing, hairstyle, posture and body movements, and other features to learn a little bit about you.

For example, let's just say your hair is highlighted orange or hot pink. The astrologer will look at you and might predict, "You are nonconforming. You like to be your own person. You don't like anyone to tell you who to be or how to act."

Now, imagine your father were to visit an astrologer. He comes dressed in a suit with a frazzled look on his face at the end of the day. The astrologer might offer, "You are a professional. You have to deal with people who are not always pleasant."

The astrologer picks up these little tidbits by looking at the client and making an educated guess. In person, the astrologer can make predictions that are more specific.

Can you think of occasions when you've looked at someone and made an educated guess about their personality or how their day was going? Probably many times. It's something we all do. We may not always be right. But sometimes we're right on target. It's not too difficult to pick up on facial expressions when someone's having a bad day. However, astrologers don't make such specific predictions in magazines, newspapers, and online. That's because they need to keep their predictions vague so as to seem true for many people.

Also, even in person the astrologer still won't usually be *too* specific. The astrologer isn't likely to suggest, "You take art lessons at Van Gogh School of Drawing"— unless, of course, you're wearing or carrying something that identifies the studio.

Covering all the bases

Another technique astrologers use is called the "rainbow ruse." This is a statement containing opposite characteristics.

An example might be, "At times you are fun loving and generous. At other times, you need your distance and are concerned with your own needs."

If you are mostly fun-loving and generous, you will probably find this true. If you are the opposite, distant and concerned with your own needs, you'll also find it familiar. And if you're a little bit of both, you'll find it very true. No matter what, the prediction or horoscope is perceived as correct.

Activity 1 – Create your own rainbow ruse

Can you come up with a prediction like the rainbow ruse that would work for everyone? Give it a try. Then test it out on family and friends to see if they think it sounds like them.

Activity 2 – What's my sign?

Are you ready for some fun? Then try this test. Read each set of descriptions below. As you read, score each word or phrase according to how well it describes you, using the scores listed below. Enter the score in the space to the right of the description.

But leave the space to the left of each number blank for now.

3 – Very much like me
2 – Somewhat like me
1 – A little like me
0 – Not at all like me

_____ 1. I am patient __, passive__, careful __, reliable__, reflective__, self-reliant__, loyal__, affectionate__, slow to anger__, solitary__.

_____ 2. I am quick minded__, analytic__, intellectual__, perceptive__, a worrier__, a loner__, self-sufficient__, outwardly unemotional__, enjoy my own companionship __, like solitary sports__.

_____ 3. I am healthy__, self-reliant__, ambitious__, eager to learn__, determined__, moody__, organized__, a planner__, practical __, thoughtful to a fault__.

_____ 4. I am dedicated to justice__, a mediator__, honest__, careful__, understanding__, compassionate__, have mood swings__, slow to make decisions__, sociable__, a friend of those in need__.

_____ 5. I am adaptive__, empathetic__, sentimental__, dual-natured (that means both sides of any characteristic)__, a fool for love__, artistic__, sometimes depressed or lazy__, imaginative__, truly known by few__, use common sense__.

_____ 6. I am capable__, ambitious__, desire to win__, courageous__, a hard worker__, generous__, extravagant__, superior__, busy__, a leader__, proud__.

_____ 7. I am genius__, near-perfect__, absentminded__, erratic__, respectful__, a people person__, charitable__, conforming__, assert my individuality__, an observer of the world__.

_____ 8. I am quiet__, introspective__, moody__, enjoy a good laugh__, curious__, resourceful__, energetic__, patriotic__, romantic__, a collector__.

_____ 9. I am always changing__, a fast talker__, dislike routine__, busy__, the life of the party __, charming__, fascinated by everything __, indecisive__, energetic__, multitasking__.

_____10. I am a leader__, courageous__, strong-willed__, witty__, optimistic__, affectionate__, a good friend__, desire to be number one__, seek challenge__, hot tempered__.

_____ 11. I am ambitious__, motivated__, intense__, aggressive__, fearless__, private__, conversationalist__, intensely emotional underneath__, calm__, an idea person__.

_____ 12. I am sharp minded__, witty__, enthusiastic__, instinctive__, a risk taker__, happy__, frank__, accepting of people's shortcomings__, magnetic__, impulsive__.

Did you score each personality trait? If not, go back and fill in any you missed. But don't spend too much time thinking about the descriptions. Just fill in the score that first comes to mind for how much or little it sounds like you.

Now, after you've scored every personality trait, add up the total score for each set of characteristics. Then put the overall score in the space to the left.

When you've finished that step, look at the next page. But don't peek until you've completed the previous steps!

What's the tally?

Now, what is the number of the set of descriptions you scored highest on? If you scored highest on number 6, for example, you fit the description of Leo.

1. Taurus
2. Virgo
3. Capricorn
4. Libra
5. Pisces
6. Leo
7. Aquarius
8. Cancer
9. Gemini
10. Aries
11. Scorpio
12. Sagittarius

Is your zodiac sign the one in which you scored highest? If not, what about your second highest score? Is that your true zodiac sign?

Keep going down the list until you find the sign that's yours according to your date of birth. If you don't remember which is your sign, turn back to the chart on page 10.

How many zodiac signs are more descriptive of you than your own? Did you score high on almost all of the descriptions? What do you suppose that might mean?

If you did score the highest on your own zodiac sign, were you already familiar with the characteristics of your sign? If so, this may have influenced the way you scored.

Of course, there is also a 1 in 12 chance you'll score highest on your own sun sign, regardless. That's the statistical odds of being the most like your own zodiac sign.

The Zodiac, you, and me

Cancer, the curious, the resourceful, and romantic
Aries, the leader, the affectionate, and optimistic
Pisces, the honest, the sentimental, and artistic
Gemini, the charming, the fascinated, and energetic

Taurus, the reliable, the reflective, and careful
Sagittarius, the instinctive, the magnetic, and cheerful
Aquarius, the charitable, the observer, and respectful
Capricorn, the self-reliant, the determined, and practical

Scorpio, the intense, the motivated, and fearless
Virgo, the wise, the self-sufficient, and analyst
Leo, the leader, the extravagant, and courageous
Libra, the just, the compassionate, and honest

Which one are you?
Which one is me?
We're each a little of all.
Wouldn't you agree?

CHAPTER 4

WHY DO SO MANY PEOPLE BELIEVE IN ASTROLOGY?

If astrology is so unreliable, why do so many people accept it as valid?

One reason is that people tend to remember only the predictions and statements that seem true. They tend to forget or disregard those that are false. In other words, people have a selective memory.

Tell me something I want to hear

Another reason people believe in the validity of horoscopes is that it makes them feel good. Astrologers are careful to mix positive qualities for each zodiac sign.

Some of the qualities for Pisces, according to one astrology website, include: idealistic, imaginative, creative, accepting, nurturing, caring, compassionate, introverted, very loving, very loyal, romantic, and spiritual."[21]

When we read positive things about ourselves, we believe them to be true. I'm a Pisces, myself. I think this sounds very much like me. But I bet it also seems like many people who are not Pisces, as well. Does the description of Pisces even sound a bit like you?

Negative readings

One psychologist has pointed out this: how many people would believe in horoscopes if they described us unfavorably? What if this was your horoscope?

Leo: You are hot-tempered and easily aggravated. Sometimes your laziness gets you into trouble. You are frequently late and show little responsibility. Others are put off by your immature ways.[22]

Would you be likely to believe this about yourself? Few people would. So, when astrologers do mention negative traits, they use careful wording—and they include plenty of good qualities to counter any bad attributes they suggest.

The looking glass self

Astrologer Robert Parry is the author of *In Defense of Astrology*. He explains, "The astrologer knows that what you become tomorrow is largely a result of how you see yourself today. You will be helped to see yourself accurately. The rest is up to you."[23]

As we've discovered, astrologers understand the way the human mind works.

The self-fulfilling prophecy

This is when the outcome of a prediction or expectation occurs as a result of being aware of the prediction or expectation. The prophecy is fulfilled by acting in a manner, often without realizing it, that makes it come true.

Behavior specialists understand our outcome is primarily based on how and what we think of ourselves. Often, when we're told something, we behave in a way that makes it come true. This is the self-fulfilling prophecy.

Astrologer Parry's comment suggests that it's the self-fulfilling prophecy that makes many astrological forecasts come true.

This explains why some people believe in astrology. They act in a manner that makes their astrological predictions come true. Then when the predictions do come true, their belief in astrology is reinforced.

For simplicity sake

Throughout the 20th century, there was considerable growth in interest in astrology. Psychologists think this is because modern society is so complex.[24] It seems people are looking for some easy answers to make their lives simpler. Today, belief in astrology continues to rise. According to the National Science Foundation, just a little more than half of all Americans believe astrology is "not at all scientific." This means almost half are either unsure whether it's scientific or believe it is in fact scientific.[25]

Today, people must make difficult decisions every day. They must decide what the best ways to invest their money are. They must also make important career decisions.

Even going to the grocery store is complex. People have to choose among a dozen brands of every item on their grocery-shopping list. They may need to compare fat, calories, sugar content, nutrition information, and prices.

Astrology offers relief from some decision-making in life. That's because according to astrology, life events are already determined.

Educational inadequacies

Finally, there is much concern that people today are undereducated in science. The world-famous astronomer Carl Sagan, author of *Contact,* who passed away in 1996, said:

"If science were explained to the average person in a way that is accessible and exciting, there would be no room for pseudoscience. But . . . in popular culture the bad science drives out the good."[26]

> **Pseudoscience** means 'false science.' Scientists believe astrology is a pseudoscience.

Sagan believed several groups are responsible for the lack of science education. First, he blamed the scientific community, to which he belonged, because it has failed to make science exciting and accessible. He was also disturbed that astrology columns are found in nearly every newspaper in America. Finally, he was concerned that America's educational system doesn't teach students how to think for themselves.[27]

Scientific knowledge of today's adults

Sagan may have been right. Do you remember I mentioned nearly half of Americans either believe astrology is scientifically based or are unsure whether it's scientific?

Astonishingly, 26% of American adults also don't know the Earth rotates around the Sun. This was the finding of a survey of 2,200 Americans by the National Science Foundation in 2012. In the same survey, 61% of American adults didn't know "that the universe began as a huge explosion." Also, more than half didn't know humans evolved from other species.[28]

CHAPTER 5

IS THERE ANY HARM IN BELIEVING IN ASTROLOGY?

It would seem astrology is a quite harmless practice. Many people who read horoscopes are undecided about astrology. These people may read horoscopes more for fun than for real advice. In such cases, it probably is harmless.

Because people may even need the simplicity it offers, there may even be some benefit. Although, it just as likely could lead people to make poor decisions in a self-fulfilling prophecy. So do the benefits outweigh the costs?

Burning a hole in pocketbooks

One problem with astrology is that some people are taken by astrologers. Many people spend much of their hard earned money on unreliable advice.

Astrology: A Big Business

- There are approximately 6,000-8,000 astrologers in the U.S.[29]
- Personal astrology services cost $60 or more for a single consultation.
- Special services such as a relationship analysis can cost $300 or more.

- In the United States, more 50 million people read their horoscopes daily.[30]
- 20 million books are sold on astrology each year.[31]
- Each year, five million Americans spend a total of 200 million dollars to speak with astrologers.[32]

That's a lot of money people are wasting on astrology considering the lack of evidence of its validity – and plenty of evidence that points to it being invalid.

When life revolves around the stars

People are not only spending large amounts of money on astrology. Some make all their decisions based on their horoscopes or astrologer's advice.

Of course, such advice isn't always bad. Much advice in horoscopes is just plain common sense. Recommendations to "invest your money wisely" and to "be patient with your children"probably never hurt.

But at other times, people may determine the fate of a meaningful relationship based on an astrological reading. They might either postpone having children or decide to have children immediately based on what their astrologer says. Other people will decide if and when to start a new business, when to visit family and friends, and even whether to go through with a necessary medical procedure, all based on their astrological readings.

Any of these situations may not be in a person's best interest depending on the person's circumstances. In fact, it can even be quite dangerous.

Astrologers also sometimes predict major events will happen. Some have predicted massive earthquakes in California in the past. Unfortunately, such predictions have led people who believed wholeheartedly in astrology to uproot their homes and families at high cost. Then, the predictions didn't even come true.[33]

Presidential predictions

One example of the danger of accepting astrology as valid is seen in a former U.S. president. President Ronald Reagan and his wife, Nancy, consulted with astrologers before he became president.

Once in office, Nancy Reagan paid a $3,000 per month retainer to consult with an astrologer. The astrologer informed Mrs. Reagan when the president should make announcements, when to take off and land in Air Force One, and the scheduling of other events.[34]

This may sound harmless and perhaps a bit silly. But for a president, it was very dangerous. Making decisions based on an unproven or invalid system and dismissing other vital factors that decisions *should* be based on could have posed life-threatening dangers to the president.

Uncritical acceptance

Another danger of astrology becomes clear when one astrologer, Robert Parry, tells readers how to deal with nonbelievers. The astrologer offers advice in his book, *In*

Defense of Astrology, to reinforce uncritical acceptance of astrology.

Personal attack

Astrologer Parry uses the elements: earth, water, air, and fire. He describes characteristics of the four different types of people who these elements are said to represent.

For example, fire types are considered aggressive and direct. They're said to have opinions on almost everything.

Air people use logic. The astrologer says they "may not be sufficiently aware of the full range of validity of astrology . . . ." These people may also use an abundance of words.[35]

As you may have concluded so far, there's no scientific evidence that astrology is valid. So, the astrologer uses a different tactic to overcome people's objections to astrology. This tactic is to verbally attack those who question astrology and to attack their personality traits.

Parry's readers learn these tactics to dismiss any criticism of astrology. Some believers in astrology learn to treat all criticism of it as character flaws in the person who makes the objection.

The unimportance of proof!?!

Parry advises his readers, "Remember always that *you* are the secure one. *You* do not need to prove anything to anybody."

He also advises believers never to tell anyone of their interest in astrology unless they are asked.[36]

These are peculiar recommendations to make for a system one is promoting as valid. The reason for such suggestions is to avoid challenges. If people who believe in astrology are never challenged, they're likely to always believe in it.

For many people, family or friends would be concerned to learn a loved one is spending their hard earned money on astrology. So by not disclosing it to family and friends, it reduces the risk of astrology being exposed for what it is (or what it is *not*).

Avoidance tactics

Do you remember Parry tells readers that if astrology is questioned to determine which of the four elements the person belongs to? Another tactic is to tell people, but then attack their "soft-spots."

With the earth type, he says to use humor, and don't appear too concerned. This will threaten the opponent and make the person feel alienated.[37]

Another option is to avoid the conversation. This means to mentally remove oneself. The believer in astrology can do this by turning their head away or digging in their pockets or purse as if busy with something else.[38]

CHAPTER 6

IS LIFE WRITTEN IN THE STARS?

Do you remember that scientists call astrology and other science look-alikes pseudoscience, or pseudopsychology? In other words, astrology resembles science or psychology but has consistently been found invalid.

In fact, the Astronomical Society of the Pacific says astrology is the field in which the most scientific experiments have been performed. This vast amount of testing has found astrology doesn't hold up to scrutiny.[39]

Whether or not astrology is valid, humans' great curiosity, imagination, and desire for magical powers did lead to an interest in science. So, astrology, or the human characteristics that led to its arrival, played an important role in the development of science.

Nietzsche on astrology

The philosopher Friedrich Nietzsche posed the following in 1886, "Do you believe then that the sciences would ever have arisen and become great if there had not before been magicians, alchemists, astrologers and wizards, who thirsted and hungered after abscondite [concealed] and

55

Remember, horoscopes can be great fun. But to *rely* on a system that has been found invalid is another story.

As much as we would all like to know what's in store for our future, many of the great surprises in life are what make it fun and worth living.

We may think we want to know our fate. But can you imagine how depressing life would be if you knew all of the sad things that would happen in your life long before they happen? Even positive events would not be as exciting and rewarding if we already knew about them.

So, the next time you read your horoscope, think about the things you've learned. Then sit back and reflect on how wonderful it is that all of life is not already written in the stars.

The Future of Me

I wish I knew what tomorrow would bring.
I wish the stars in the heavens could sing.

Tell me, please, what my future does hold.
What will I be?
Will I grow old?

Tell me, please, do the planets hold the key?
Would I like what I'm told?
Or do I really want to see?

CHAPTER 7

EXPLORING ON YOUR OWN

If you're still uncertain about astrology, or if you'd like more evidence of its invalidity to share with others, there are many ways to examine astrology yourself. Try these fun, informative activities.

Activity 3 – Which horoscope is mine?

Pick up a newspaper or magazine or go online and read the horoscopes of all the zodiac signs for the previous day or the last month. Highlight each sentence under each zodiac sign that seems accurate for you.

After you have read all twelve horoscopes, count how many besides your own seemed right for you.

Likely, several horoscopes sound as much like you or your day as your own. You might even find one or several are more accurate than your own horoscope. This is because astrologers use vague statements or predictions that apply to a large number of people.

Activity 4 – Astrology online

Do an Internet search using the following phrase: "today's horoscopes." You should get oodles of results directing you to websites where you can read your horoscope online.

Visit several websites and search for the horoscope for your zodiac sign. If your parents approve, print your horoscope from 10 or 15 sites.

Next, read each of the horoscopes. Do any contradict each other?

Note also that some of the horoscopes may be identical. If so, that's because some horoscope writers syndicate their horoscope columns. This means horoscopes written by the same writer or astrologer appear in more than one publication or website.

Activity 5 – A stab in the dark

Clip the horoscopes from a magazine. Then, cut off the zodiac sign, and assign a letter to each. Be sure to make a list of which letter you assigned to which horoscope or zodiac sign.

On the last day of the month, interview family and friends. Ask each person which of the 12 horoscopes most fits that person for the previous month.

Log the letter of the horoscope that each person chooses. Also, don't forget to make a note of the person's birth date and zodiac sign next to the letter of the horoscope they chose.

Once you've gathered several people's choices, compare each choice to their actual zodiac sign. Did anyone choose their own zodiac sign? If so, how many? How many were wrong?

Do this same test again at the end of next month.

This time, compare the sign that each person chooses to the one he or she chose the previous month.

Did any of your subjects choose the same sun sign as they did the month before? How many picked their own sign this time? What does this tell you?

Activity 6 – A real study

Try to duplicate the following study, and see if you get the same or similar results as the researcher who performed it initially.

For the next few weeks, carry this personality profile with you, and read it to as many people as you can.

> You have a strong need for other people to like you and for them to admire you. You have a tendency to be critical of yourself. You have a great deal of unused energy which you have not turned to your advantage. While you have some personality weaknesses, you are generally able to compensate for them. . . . Disciplined and controlled on the outside, you tend to be worrisome and insecure inside. At times you have serious doubts as to whether you have made the right decision or done the right thing. You prefer a certain amount of change and variety and become dissatisfied when hemmed in by restrictions and limitations. You pride yourself on being an

independent thinker and do not accept other opinions without satisfactory proof. You have found it unwise to be too frank in revealing yourself to others. At times you are extraverted, affable, sociable, while at other times you are introverted, wary, and reserved. Some of your aspirations tend to be pretty unrealistic.[40]

Afterward, ask each person to rate how well the profile describes him or herself. Your subjects should choose one of the following ratings: excellent, good, average, or poor. Make a list of these four choices and put a tally mark next to the description that is chosen.

Remember not to let your subject see your worksheet. Otherwise, your subject might base their response on the marks that have already been recorded.

When you've finished, total the number of people who selected each description.

When the horoscope was read to 79 college students in the original study, these were the ratings:

29 students said it was an excellent description

30 students said it was a good description

15 students said it was average

5 students said it was poor.[41]

This profile should have only described 6 or 7 students. That's the number when dividing the total number of students in the study (79) by the 12 zodiac signs. Instead, the profile reasonably described 74 of the students.[42]

Why do you think the profile fits so many people? Reread it a couple of times and see if you can figure it out. When you think you have the answer, turn to page 64, and compare your conclusions.

Activity 7 – Tell me something specific!

To learn more about the accuracy of horoscopes, try this fun experiment, and track your horoscopes using the log that follows.

Each time you read your horoscope, write each prediction on a separate line. At the end of the day, note whether each prediction or statement is true, false, or depends.

Track your horoscopes for several days or weeks. When you 've finished, count how many predictions were true, false, and depended upon how you perceived them.

Then go back and review those that you marked as true. You'll probably discover the predictions that did seem right were vague. In other words, they were lacking in detail and could have been valid for many people regardless of their zodiac sign.

Example:

DATE	PREDICTION	ACCURACY
July 6	You'll get a big surprise.	False
July 6	You're prone to accidents today.	True

Answers to Activity 6

A) The reason this profile describes so many people is that most of the characteristics include the opposite trait as well. It reflects both:

- extraverted *and* introverted
- self-doubt *and* pride in independent thinking
    – "disciplined and controlled" *versus* "worrisome and insecure."

B) Another reason is that positive characteristics are intertwined. People want to believe positive things that are said about them.

C) A third reason is that people remember the characteristics that are accurate and tend to forget the inaccuracies.

Want to read more books in the *Sleuthing For Explanations* series?

Visit www.greengrovepress.com/sleuthing/ and sign up to be notified when new books in this series are released.

More Reading

If you found this book fun and helpful in understanding astrology, here are some other books you might like about science and pseudoscience.

Alexander Fox & the Amazing Mind Reader by John Clayton. Grades 3+

Bill Nye the Science Guy: Pseudoscience video.

Bringing UFOs Down to Earth by Philip J. Klass. Grades 4 to 7

Encyclopedia of Pseudoscience: From Alien Abductions to Zone Therapy by William F. Williams. Grades 7+

Flat Earth? Round Earth? by Theresa Martin.

How Come? Every Kid's Science Questions Explained by Kathy Wollard and Debra Solomon. Grades 4 to 6

How Do You Know It's True? Discovering the Difference Between Science and Superstition by Hy Ruchlis. Grades 7 to 10

How to Fake a Moon Landing: Exposing the Myths of Science Denial by Darryl Cunningham. Grades 7+

Junior Skeptic by Daniel Loxton. Magazine bound inside *Skeptic Magazine.*

The Little Book of Big Questions by Jackie French and Martha Newbigging. Grades 3 to 7

The Magic Detectives: Join Them in Solving Strange Mysteries by Joe Nickell. Grades 4 to 6

Maybe Yes, Maybe No: A Guide for Young Skeptics by Dan Barker. Grades 4 to 7

Nibbling on Einstein's Brain: The Good, the Bad and the Bogus in Science by Diane Swanson and Francis Blake. Grades 3 to 7

Wonder-Workers! How They Perform the Impossible by Joe Nickell. Grades 4 to 6

Sasquatches from Outer Space: Exploring the Weirdest Mysteries Ever by Tim Yule. Grades 4 to 7.

Science in a Nanosecond: Illustrated Answers to 100 Basic Science Questions James A. Haught. Grades 4 to 6

Science Versus Pseudoscience by Nathan Aeseng. Grades 7+

Test Your Psychic Powers by Susan Blackmore & Adam Hart-Davis. Grades 7+

GLOSSARY

Astrology - The study of how the movements of the sun, moon, planets, and stars influence human behavior and events.

Constellation – A pattern of stars.

Horoscopes - The charts that are used by astrologers that show the position of the planets and the stars at particular times. Also, the astrological forecasts that you read in magazines and newspapers.

Omen astrology – An ancient form of astrology in which only major events were predicted.

Pseudopsychology – False psychology.

Pseudoscience – False science.

Zodiac – An invisible path in the sky that extends through the 12 constellations of the zodiac. Also, a diagram that represents the signs of the zodiac.

ABOUT THE AUTHOR

Kimberly Blaker is an author and freelance writer and has been published in more than 200 magazines on a variety of topics ranging from parenting and family life to health and lifestyle. Kimberly is also a skeptic, particularly when it comes to horoscopes, mind reading, alien abductions, ghosts, and numerous other claims for which there's no scientific evidence. She hopes to enlighten readers on these and other topics by evaluating with them the evidence, or lack thereof, and providing readers the tools to make their own determinations.

INDEX

¹NOTES

_https://www.dailyom.com/cgi-bin/display/articledisplay.cgi?aid=60412

² Grant Lewi, Astrology for the Millions, (St. Paul: Llewellyn Publications, 2002), preface.

³ https://books.google.com/books?
id=i2Nm8OyXpyQC&pg=PA223&lpg=PA223&dq=1979+studies+astrology+i
ntroversion+extroversion&source=bl&ots=K0zxRqbb3o&sig=4lOQp0ICsYh7
29pRTTjDyhJyxcI&hl=en&sa=X&ved=0ahUKEwigkOLMmf3YAhUq_IMK
HdkzD3kQ6AEISDAE#v=onepage&q=1979%20studies%20astrology
%20introversion%20extroversion&f=false p. 223

⁴ https://books.google.com/books?
id=i2Nm8OyXpyQC&pg=PA223&lpg=PA223&dq=1979+studies+astrology+i
ntroversion+extroversion&source=bl&ots=K0zxRqbb3o&sig=4lOQp0ICsYh7
29pRTTjDyhJyxcI&hl=en&sa=X&ved=0ahUKEwigkOLMmf3YAhUq_IMK
HdkzD3kQ6AEISDAE#v=onepage&q=1979%20studies%20astrology
%20introversion%20extroversion&f=false p. 223

⁵ https://books.google.com/books?
id=d57WiB38aTMC&pg=PA51&lpg=PA51&dq=pawlick+1979+astrology+int
roversion&source=bl&ots=MHGGuUhlMM&sig=JNvH1iP82R773nw1v1h60
4k03YM&hl=en&sa=X&ved=0ahUKEwiY9tmIof3YAhVG74MKHVVJCnY
Q6AEIMTAB#v=onepage&q=pawlick%201979%20astrology
%20introversion&f=false p. 51

⁶ https://books.google.com/books?
id=i2Nm8OyXpyQC&pg=PA223&lpg=PA223&dq=1979+studies+astrology+i
ntroversion+extroversion&source=bl&ots=K0zxRqbb3o&sig=4lOQp0ICsYh7
29pRTTjDyhJyxcI&hl=en&sa=X&ved=0ahUKEwigkOLMmf3YAhUq_IMK
HdkzD3kQ6AEISDAE#v=onepage&q=1979%20studies%20astrology
%20introversion%20extroversion&f=false p. 223

⁷ https://books.google.com/books?
id=JOpq1LOGrr0C&pg=PA219&lpg=PA219&dq=eysenck+studies+introversi
on+astrology+AND+%22no+correlation%22&source=bl&ots=_8U6wbIOW-
&sig=XLZGdpUpZQ6zsgw9loP3GVMaQx0&hl=en&sa=X&ved=0ahUKEwj
u2obEpv3YAhXk4IMKHWUnCG8Q6AEIKTAA#v=onepage&q=eysenck
%20studies%20introversion%20astrology%20AND%20%22no%20correlation
%22&f=false p. 219

⁸ https://skepsis.nl/mars-effect/

⁹ https://skepsis.nl/mars-effect/

¹⁰ https://skepsis.nl/mars-effect/

¹¹ http://www.skepsis.no/english/subject/astrology/studies.html

¹² Several sources were used to get all the details of this one study.

[13] https://www.washingtonpost.com/news/wonk/wp/2015/06/15/what-your-birth-month-means-for-your-risk-of-disease/?utm_term=.2bf0d009224a

[14] Grant Lewi, Astrology for the Millions, (St. Paul: Llewellyn Publications, 1996), preface.

[15] https://books.google.com/books?id=aC8Baky2qTcC&pg=PA67&lpg=PA67&dq=voas+study+astrology+marriage&source=bl&ots=yILKDle6DZ&sig=zJIuZPVyeMnmN5Sbgv5xOO6jX3s&hl=en&sa=X&ved=0ahUKEwjfye38xf3YAhVM9YMKHaTzC20Q6AEIQTAE#v=onepage&q=voas%20study%20astrology%20marriage&f=false p. 67

[16] Carl Sagan, The Demon-Haunted World (New York: Random House, 1995), 242.

[17] http://www.skepsis.no/english/subject/astrology/studies.html

[18] https://www.cengage.com/resource_uploads/static_resources/053439549X/1660/chapter04.html

[19] Nathan Aaseng, Science Versus Superstion, (New York: Franklin Watts, 1994), 108.

[20] Brown, Kourtni.; Husted, Mandy. Fraknoi, Andrew, "Ask Astro: Astronomy versus Astrology, Meteors," Astronomy v. 27 no1 (Jan. 1999) p. 102-3 [online] [cited 9 September 2002]; available at http://firstsearch.oclc.org/WebZ/FTFETCH?sessionid=sp03sw11-53815-d41awl1ip9ep1t:entitypagenum=16:0:rule=990:fetchtype=fulltext:dbname=WilsonSelectPlus_FT:recno=20:resultset=6:ftformat=ASCII:format=T:isbillable=TRUE:numrecs=1:isdirectarticle=FALSE:entityemailfullrecno=20:entityemailfullresultset=6:entityemailftfrom=WilsonSelectPlus_FT:

[21] http://www.compatible-astrology.com/pisces-traits.html

[22] Used this idea from Dennis Coon, Introduction to Psychology: Exploration and Application (Minneapolis: West Publishing Company, 1995), 30.

[23] Robert Parry, In Defense of Astrology, (Foulsham & Co. Ltd., 2005), 58.

[24] Willard A. Heaps, Superstition, (Nashville: Thomas Nelson Inc., Publishers, 1972), 106.

[25] https://www.nsf.gov/statistics/seind14/index.cfm/chapter-7/c7h.htm

[26] https://archive.org/stream/BurdenOfSkepticism-CarlSagan/burdenofskeptism_djvu.txt

[27] https://archive.org/stream/BurdenOfSkepticism-CarlSagan/burdenofskeptism_djvu.txt

[28] https://www.npr.org/sections/thetwo-way/2014/02/14/277058739/1-in-4-americans-think-the-sun-goes-around-the-earth-survey-says

[29] http://www.telegraph.co.uk/culture/3573123/Twenty-facts-about-astrology.html

[30] https://www.the-scientist.com/?articles.view/articleNo/10249/title/Top-Scientists-Must-Fight-Astrology-Or-All-Of-Us-Will-Face-The-Consequences/

[31] Life, found in Judith Hayes, Skeptical Inquirer, "Starkle, Starkle, Little Twink," September/October 1998

[32] https://www.the-scientist.com/?articles.view/articleNo/10249/title/Top-Scientists-Must-Fight-Astrology-Or-All-Of-Us-Will-Face-The-Consequences/

[33] Gary Jennings, *The Teenager's Realistic Guide to Astrology*, (New York: Association Press, 1971), 221.

[34] https://www.hollywoodreporter.com/news/sister-nancy-reagan-astrologer-nancy-873339

[35] Robert Parry, In Defense of Astrology, (Foulsham & Co. Ltd., 2005), 65-66.

[36] Robert Parry, In Defense of Astrology, (Foulsham & Co. Ltd., 2005), 68.

[37] Robert Parry, In Defense of Astrology, (Foulsham & Co. Ltd., 2005), 69.

[38] Robert Parry, In Defense of Astrology, (Foulsham & Co. Ltd., 2005), 69-70.

[39] http://www.astrosociety.org/education/resources/pseudobib.html#1

[40] R.E. Ulrich, T.J. Stachnik, and N.R. Stainton, "Student acceptance of generalized personality interpretations," Psychological Report, 13, 1963, 831-34.

[41] R.E. Ulrich, T.J. Stachnik, and N.R. Stainton, "Student acceptance of generalized personality interpretations," Psychological Report, 13, 1963, 831-34.

[42] R.E. Ulrich, T.J. Stachnik, and N.R. Stainton, "Student acceptance of generalized personality interpretations," Psychological Report, 13, 1963, 831-34. cited in Dennis Coon, Introduction to Psychology: Exploration and Application (Minneapolis: West Publishing Company, 1995), 30.

CPSIA information can be obtained
at www.ICGtesting.com
Printed in the USA
BVHW03*0039280418
514697BV00005B/24/P